LOOK, SEE, FIND ME

For you, Rainer.

For all of life's discoveries we shared together.

With a lifetime of love. S

A catalogue record for this
book is available from the
National Library of Australia

ISBN: 9781486319886 (hbk)
ISBN: 9781486321599 (pbk)
ISBN: 9781486319893 (epdf)
ISBN: 9781486319909 (epub)

Published by:
CSIRO Publishing
36 Gardiner Road, Clayton VIC 3168
Private Bag 10, Clayton South VIC 3169
Australia

Telephone: +61 3 9545 8400
Email: publishing.sales@csiro.au
Website: www.publish.csiro.au
Sign up to our email alerts: publish.csiro.au/earlyalert

Edited by Belinda Bolliger
Cover, text design and layout by MDCN Creative
Printed by Ingram Lightning Source

CSIRO acknowledges the Traditional Owners of the lands that we live and work on across Australia and pays its respect
to Elders past and present. CSIRO recognises that Aboriginal and Torres Strait Islander peoples have made and will
continue to make extraordinary contributions to all aspects of Australian life including culture, economy and science.
The use of Western science in this publication should not be interpreted as diminishing the knowledge
of plants, animals and environment from Indigenous ecological knowledge systems.

With thanks to Shane Ahyong, Michelle Gleeson, Peter Last, Peter Menkhorst and Mike Swan for their comments.

Note for readers: A glossary can be found at the back of the book.

Note for teachers: Teacher notes are available at: https://www.publish.csiro.au/book/8211/#forteachers

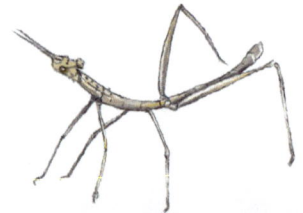

LOOK, SEE, FIND ME

SANDRA SEVERGNINI

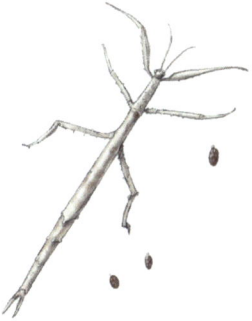

CSIRO
PUBLISHING

The world is full of mystery,
so much to learn,
so much to see.

I see you, but can you see me,

hiding up here, in the tree?

And what about me?

Western screech-owl
(*Megascops kennicottii*)

Pandora pinemoth
(*Coloradia pandora*)

This branch is full of leaves of green,
hiding here we can't be seen . . .

Or can we?

European mantis
(*Mantis religiosa*)

Great green bush-cricket
(*Tettigonia viridissima*)

We're sitting still without a sound.
Look really close,

can we be found?

Panther chameleon
(*Furcifer pardalis*)

Jewelled chameleon
(*Furcifer campani*)

Parson's chameleon
(*Calumma parsonii*)

I'm on the flower, I blend in well.

If you see me here, would you tell?

Goldenrod crab spider
(*Misumena vatia*)

Hidden in dead leaves on the ground,

can you see us hopping around?

Black-spotted sticky frog
(*Kalophrynus pleurostigma*)

Malayan horned frog
(*Megophrys nasuta*)

We're shaped like sticks to hide from prey.

As the wind blows, we rock and sway.

Tessellated stick insect
(*Anchiale austrotessulata*)

Crowned stick insect
(*Onchestus rentzi*)

Titan stick insect
(*Acrophylla titan*)

Among the moss and leaves we rest.

It's where we camouflage the best.

Eyelash leaf-tailed gecko
(*Uroplatus phantasticus*)

Mossy leaf-tailed gecko
(*Uroplatus sikorae*)

I'm like an orchid, can you see?

Look very hard, which one is me?

Orchid mantis
(*Hymenopus coronatus*)

As the dead leaves flutter from the sky,

can you tell which one am I?

Orange oakleaf butterfly
(*Kallima inachus*)

Among the coral where we dwell,
our knobbly skin blends in well.

Pygmy seahorses
(*Hippocampus bargibanti*)

Denise's pygmy seahorses
(*Hippocampus denise*)

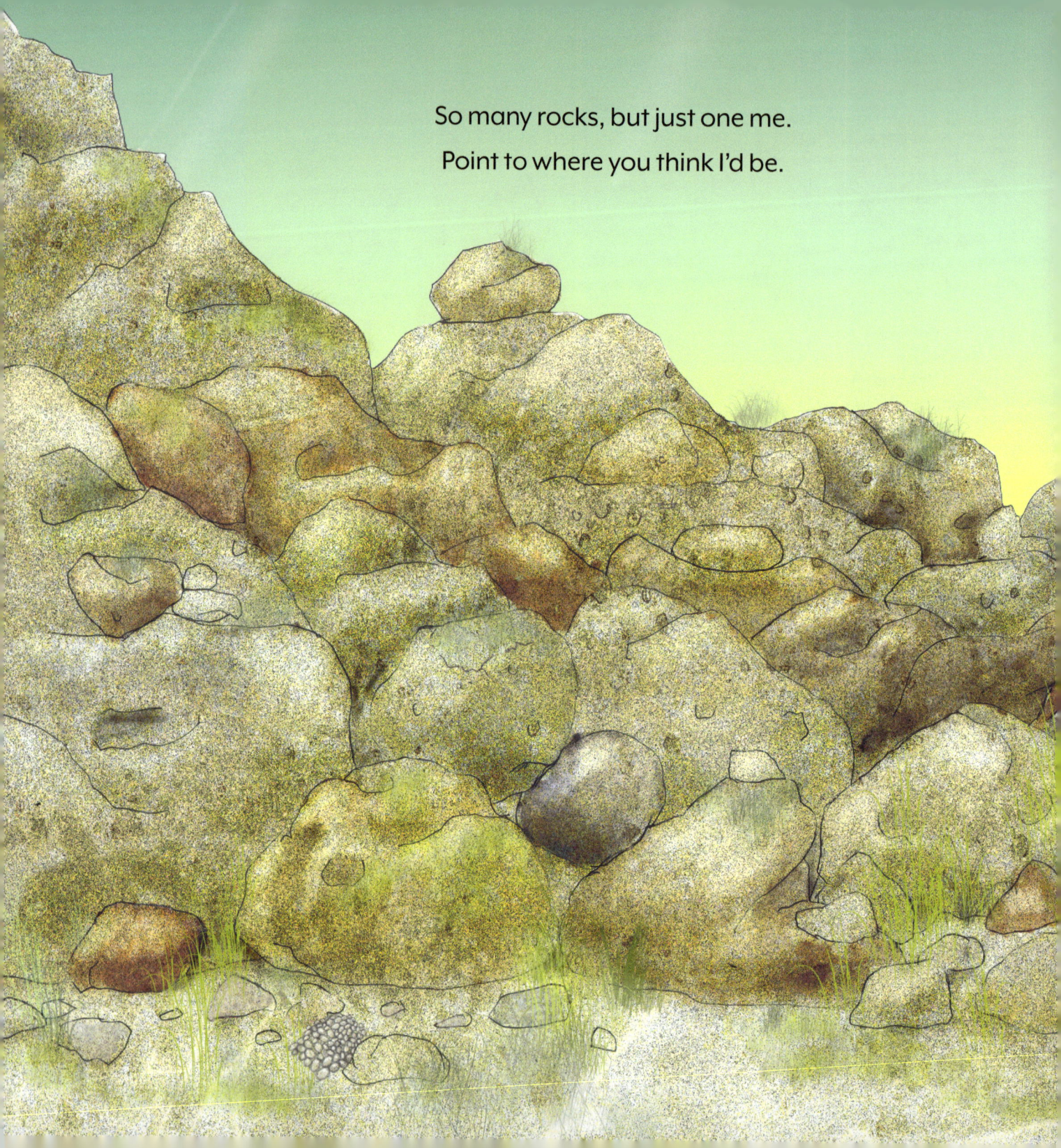

So many rocks, but just one me.

Point to where you think I'd be.

Estuarine stonefish
(*Synanceia horrida*)

Hidden among the sand and shell,
our textured skins hide us well.

Three twinspot flounder
(*Pseudorhombus dupliciocellatus*)

Pharaoh cuttlefish
(*Sepia pharaonis*)

We use plants, sponges and anything ornate,
to camouflage and decorate.

Corallimorph decorator crab
(*Cyclocoeloma tuberculata*)

Sponge crab
(*Lauridromia dehaani*)

Jewelled hermit crab
(*Dardanus gemmatus*)

MEET THE CAMOUFLAGED CREATURES

Western screech-owl
(*Megascops kennicottii*)

Common across western North America, these small owls rest in tree hollows or, if resting in the open, can flatten their feathers to blend in with the tree bark. They are around 19 to 25 centimetres in height. The males are smaller than the females.

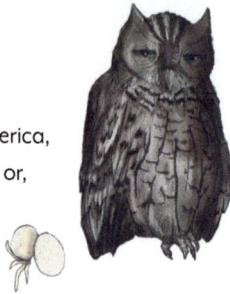

European mantis
(*Mantis religiosa*)

European mantises are also known as praying mantises because the position of their front legs makes them look like they are praying. They are one of the most common mantises in Europe and North America. Their camouflage changes during their life cycle: eggs look like seeds, juveniles resemble ants and adults disguise themselves as leaves or sticks. Males are around 7 centimetres long while females are around 8 centimetres long.

Panther chameleon
(*Furcifer pardalis*)
Jewelled chameleon (*Furcifer campani*)
Parson's chameleon (*Calumma parsonii*)

These colourful chameleons are all native to Madagascar. They can change colour to adapt to their surroundings when they are stressed or under threat, or to respond to a change in light or temperature.

Pandora pinemoth
(*Coloradia pandora*)

Native to western North America, these moths live in pine tree forests. Their brown and green colouring allows them to blend into their surroundings. They lay groups of eggs on pine needles or on the trunk of the tree. An adult pinemoth's wingspan is usually between 7 and 10 centimetres.

Great green bush-cricket
(*Tettigonia viridissima*)

This large bush-cricket is around 4 to 7 centimetres long, with females longer than males. Their antennae can be very long – often up to three times their body length. They can be found across most of Europe.

Goldenrod crab spider
(*Misumena vatia*)

Found across North America, Europe and parts of Asia, this spider uses its body colour to disguise itself among flower heads. This allows the spider to catch unsuspecting insects that land on the flower to find pollen, but instead find themselves becoming a tasty snack. The female lays her eggs in a silken sac attached to the leaves of the plant.

Black-spotted sticky frog (*Kalophrynus pleurostigma*)
Malayan horned frog (*Megophrys nasuta*)

Both found in South-east Asia, these frogs disguise themselves among the leaf litter on the forest floor. Eggs can be laid in small areas of water, often underneath leaves, rocks and logs. The Malayan horned frog uses camouflage to find its food, hiding in the leaves until an insect, lizard or even another frog comes past, then jumping out to gulp down its meal!

Tessellated stick insect
(*Anchiale austrotessulata*)
Crowned stick insect
(*Onchestus rentzi*)
Titan stick insect (*Acrophylla titan*)

Found in Australia, these insects use camouflage to blend in with surrounding leaves and sticks. The tessellated and crowned stick insects are between 12 and 15 centimetres in length, while the titan stick insect can grow up to 26 centimetres, making it one of the longest insects in Australia. The females do not keep their eggs in the plant where they are laid, but instead flick them down to the ground.

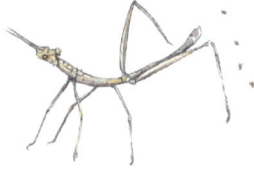

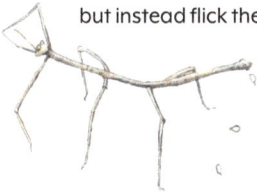

Eyelash leaf-tailed gecko
(*Uroplatus phantasticus*)
Mossy leaf-tailed gecko
(*Uroplatus sikorae*)

The eyelash leaf-tailed gecko has two eyelash-like horns and a tail with a leaf-like appearance. These features help it blend into its surroundings and hunt for prey. It can grow up to 9 centimetres in length, including the tail. Mossy leaf-tailed geckos can be up to 20 centimetres long and have flaps of skin along their body, head and limbs, which make their outline almost invisible when at rest. They can also change their skin colour. Both of these geckos are endemic to Madagascar and the females of both species lay eggs under leaves or leaf litter.

Orchid mantis
(*Hymenopus coronatus*)

Found in South-east Asia, the orchid mantis can mimic (or copy) parts of the orchid flower. Their four walking legs resemble flower petals and the toothed front pair is used for grasping prey. Their brilliant colouring can change between pink and brown to adapt to the background. They can lay over 100 eggs on branches or leaves.

Orange oakleaf butterfly
(*Kallima inachus*)

When its wings are closed, the orange oakleaf butterfly looks exactly like a dried autumn leaf. It doesn't just mimic the colouring of a dead leaf, but also the shape, the midrib and even the veins. Found across tropical Asia, its wingspan ranges from 8.5 to 11 centimetres. Eggs are laid in batches on oak leaves.

Pygmy seahorse
(*Hippocampus bargibanti*)
Denise's pygmy seahorse
(*Hippocampus denise*)

Found in the Indo-Pacific region, these tiny seahorses cling to coral with their curly tails and mimic the colours and textures of the coral so well that they are hard to see. At around 2 centimetres in size, the males of these species brood the eggs in a pouch for 2 to 4 weeks before giving birth.

Corallimorph decorator crab
(*Cyclocoeloma tuberculata*)
Sponge crab
(*Lauridromia dehaani*)
Jewelled hermit crab
(*Dardanus gemmatus*)

These crabs are found in the Indo-Pacific region. They select pieces of seaweed, coral, rocks or even other small animals from around their habitat and then carry them on the back of their shells. This camouflage helps the crabs look nearly invisible on the reef or seabed, protecting them from predators. Female crabs carry their eggs under their abdomens.

Estuarine stonefish
(*Synanceia horrida*)
Three twinspot flounder
(*Pseudorhombus dupliciocellatus*)
Pharaoh cuttlefish
(*Sepia pharaonis*)

These three species, found in the Indo-West Pacific region, are all experts in camouflage. The estuarine stonefish is one of the world's most venomous fish. Its brownish to reddish-orange colouring helps it blend into its rocky habitat, making it harder for predators to spot and giving it an advantage in capturing prey. It grows up to 60 centimetres and lays its eggs on the seabed.

With its unique flat body, the three twinspot flounder hides in muddy and sandy environments, which is both a defence mechanism against predators and helps to ambush prey. This flounder can spawn up to a million eggs that are carried along by currents.

Pharaoh cuttlefish are molluscs which can grow up to 42 centimetres. They are masters of camouflage, changing their colour and texture to blend into their surroundings. They lay their eggs in rock crevices.

MORE ABOUT CAMOUFLAGE

Animals use camouflage to change their appearance, helping them to survive, find food and avoid being eaten. Camouflage can also help attract a mate, protect eggs or young, or communicate, such as warning when danger is nearby.

One of the main ways animals camouflage themselves is by changing their colour. This can be done gradually, such as changing colour between seasons as the animal adjusts to temperature, the amount of daylight and habitat changes. Colour change can also happen very quickly in response to danger or stress. Some animals change not only their colour but also their patterns and markings to increase their disguise. This helps them to blend into their surroundings so they are hidden from predators or even appear to be something far less appealing, such as a poisonous species or even poo!

Animals can also camouflage themselves by changing their shape, behaviour or even their smell. There are geckos and butterflies that change to look like a leaf, and octopuses that fit into the tiniest of spaces. Some animals use the smell of other species, including plants, to hide their scent. Decorator crabs attach parts of their habitat to their shells to disguise themselves under their decorations.

GLOSSARY

Abdomen: the back part of an insect's body, found behind the head and the thorax; the thorax is the middle part of the body that holds the legs and wings (if any are present).

Antennae: long, thin sensors on the head of an insect or crustacean.

Endemic: only found in one place, native to that place.

Habitat: the place where a plant or animal lives with everything it needs, including water, food and shelter.

Midrib: the central vein of a leaf, running from the base to the tip.

Native: a plant or animal that has existed naturally in an area for thousands of years.

Predator: an animal that hunts, kills and eats other animals.

Prey: animals that are hunted and eaten by other animals.

Species: a group of living things that have similar characteristics and can breed with each other to produce young that can also successfully breed.

www.ingramcontent.com/pod-product-compliance
Lightning Source LLC
Chambersburg PA
CBHW042011080426

42734CB00002B/49